*Mau 17/97*

*For [...]
Believ[...]
are [...]
fame, fortune, health,
happiness and love!*

*Nattalia Lea*

# Miracles for the Entrepreneur

### A word about the author and illustrator:

**Nattalia Lea** graduated from the University of British Columbia in 1978 with a bio-resources engineering degree (electives in fine arts) and from the British Columbia Institute of Technology in bio-sciences technology in 1973. Her artwork has been shown at juried art exhibitions in Vancouver and Calgary. Prior to becoming an accomplished Calgary-based freelance writer and consultant, she worked eight years as an engineer. Her articles have appeared in newspapers and magazines in Canada, the United States, Malaysia and Singapore -- *The Globe and Mail, Profit, Oilweek, Business in Calgary, Vancouver Sun, Victoria Times Colonist, Canadian Lawyer, CA Magazine, Alberta Report,* etc. Ms. Lea has spoken publicly on journalism, entrepreneurship and international marketing; and been a guest on *CBC Newsworld, Vancouver's Dave Abbott AM 1040 Show* and other radio shows. She is a nominee for inclusion in the 1997 edition of *Who's Who of Canadian Women*. In her spare time, she is cartooning her next book, *The Revenge of the Computer Widow.*

# Miracles for the Entrepreneur

*Written & Illustrated By Nattalia Lea*

PLATYPUS PUBLISHERS,
Calgary, Alberta, Canada

The writer/illustrator wishes to thank all the entrepreneurs she has reported on (as a journalist), and to whom this book is dedicated. She also thanks friends, relatives and three particularly close associates who have driven her up the wall, and more or less, kept her there. Special thanks to globetrotting geologists Godfried Wasser and Doug Esson at Eucalyptus Consulting Inc. for their editing assistance, when grounded in Calgary.

All originals for cartoons were hand drawn by pen with plastic film shading overlays.
All characters have been trademarked. All rights reserved.
All characters in this book are fictional and any resemblance to actual persons and animals, living or dead, is entirely coincidental.

No part of this book may be used or reproduced in any manner whatsoever, without written consent from the publisher, with the exception of reprints in the context of reviews. For information, write to:
**Platypus Publishers,**
2323E 3rd Ave. N.W.,
Calgary, AB. T2N 0K9 Canada
Tel: (403) 283-0498 Fax: (403) 270-3023 E-Mail: eucalypt@cadvision.com
Internet: http://www.cadvision.com/Home_Pages/accounts/eucalypt/Home.html

Copyright © Nattalia Lea, 1996
All rights reserved.
Printed on Recycled Paper in Canada
First Printing May 1996
Second Printing October 1996

Canadian Cataloguing in Publication Data

Lea, Nattalia
    Miracles for the entrepreneur

ISBN 0-96998-640-8

1. Businessmen-Caricatures and cartoons. 2. Canadian wit and humor, Pictorial. I. Title
NC1449.L42A4 1996     741.5'971     C95-910253-4

# TABLE OF CONTENTS

| | | |
|---|---|---:|
| Introduction | | 1 |
| I. | The Great Corporate Rat Race | 3 |
| II. | From Employee to Entrepreneur | 17 |
| III. | In Business | 31 |
| IV. | And They Lived Happily Ever After | 57 |
| V. | Entrepreneurs - The Next Generation | 79 |
| Epilogue | | 87 |

# Introduction

In the beginning, there was a quiet little rat named Joe. In fact, so silent, nobody would ever hear a peep out of him, unless he burped on the elevator and said out loud, "Excuse me!" Joe started working for XYZ Corp. in the mailroom after high school. His retired father, a senior bean counter at XYZ Corp., got him the job. When Joe turned 21, he married his high school sweetheart, a rat named Babe and worked at XYZ Corp. to put her through law school. They now have two children — a seven year-old daughter, Ratilla (so-named after Atilla the Hun) and four-year-old son, B. Rat.

It's been 21 years since Joe has stepped foot at XYZ Corp. Babe has graduated from law school and works for a downtown law firm. Joe's gone to night school and got his official diploma in bean counting. He no longer runs around XYZ Corp. in flighty sneakers and in a T-shirt that says politically incorrect statements. Instead, he's in a three-piece pin-striped suit, polished shoes and a tie that he claims, cuts off the circulation to his brain.

Joe's fast approaching the big 4-0 and Babe's not far behind, by about 40 days and 40 nights. And what does he have to show? Well, there's an inside office, membership at the local bean counters club and subscription to XYZ Corp. newsletter. But darn, if he's ever going to be somebody at XYZ Corp., he needs to mutate into a turkey. And he's never heard of a rat undergoing gene therapy to become a grumpy bird that can't fly.

Read on and enjoy *Miracles for the Entrepreneur*, a world where a zoo full of animals learn the art of becoming billionaires. Joe's not the only one contemplating his navel at XYZ Corp., ready for a career crisis. There's Rose Lard, a portly pig, in the legal department, recently divorced with a ten year-old daughter. Elsewhere in cowtown where Joe and Babe Rat reside, there's a fed up Celine Le Friesen at Holstein & Holstein, Joe's Brother Pete and a herd of country folks, moving in to saviour urban life.

# The Great Corporate Rat Race

| | | | |
|---|---|---|---|
| **Thomas Turkey Sr.™**, Founder, XYZ Corp. | **Terminator X™**, Bank of Bozo C.E.O. | **Thomas Turkey Jr.™**, C.E.O., XYZ Corp. | **Timothy Turkey™**, President, XYZ Corp. |
| **Gina Alien™**, Pion Customer Service | **Merv Mole™**, Pion Bank Teller | **Felix Fat Cat™**, Pion, National taxation | **Cornelius Friesen™**, Pion, CIA Agent |
| **Guaca Mole™**, Pion, Computer Nerd | **Fran Feline™**, Pion, Executive Assist. | **Rose Lard™**, Pion Legal Counsel | **Joe Rat™**, Pion Bean Counter |

# If You Work For A Turkey
## (or why I became an entrepreneur)
### *By Joe Rat*

Corporate rats race up the career ladder to timers that tell them how successfully they've made their bosses look good. But even trained rats can't succeed if they work, as so many do, for a real turkey. Like the ones who read the newspaper with their eyes closed. Or Real Bosses who regularly use four letter words that start with "f" to blame you for what they did wrong.

Welcome to World War III, with stress as its most dreaded weapon. Here you encounter bug-eyed business rats – lean from aerobics and other lithe lycra-clad sports. Mean because aggression comes with the territory. Worse still are the "executroid strains" who carry the plague. These rats have been bred to produce stress in other, lesser rats by attacking their subordinates with grueling demands. At the center of the universe, scheduling meetings to their whims, they wonder why everybody below them is so uptight.

A little bit of pressure at work helps keep your edge, but who settles for just a little in today's corporate rat race? "It's all in your mind," says one stress management expert. "Coping with stress is an individual's legacy."

The myth, consistently proven wrong over the past 15 years, is that chief executive officers (alias turkeys) are under a lot of stress. The reality is that those who perceive that they lack control on the job are the ones who encounter the most stress and frustration – the secretaries, the assembly-line workers, the bean counters (like I was once upon a time) and many others. But you can be high on the career ladder and feel just as much lack of control – and resulting stress – if your boss is a real turkey.

Upper echelon executroids claim that better time management is what stressed-out subordinates need. Sure, just work at fever pitch for 16 hours a day to meet these time pressures.

But few of us handle stress well these days, whatever the demands. The war on stress is not over until self-imposed pressures are liberated. Perfectionism and over-achievement are some grenades to throw away. "Baby boomers are taught they can have it all," says my shrink.

The me-first attitude, an affliction of Yuppies, is killing North American work productivity as inter-personal conflicts create office cutthroats and other mutants. Instead of information sharing at work, information is often withheld, creating stress for others.

And there's often little release at home for the corporate rat, especially, the common dual-income family rat (like me, Babe, Ratilla and B.Rat). According to a renown respectable research organization, dual-income spouses typically spend 13 minutes in meaningful conversation daily.

We rush to work, rush to daycares, rush to night classes and rush to exercise. Rat traps cater to the AAA-rated stress personalities. Adventure travel firms charge thousands of dollars to take business rats and clones on ordeals that will fill their need for punishment as they trek up Everest or cross the Sahara on a camel. In the trenches, the wounded succumb to drugs, alcohol, and caffeine abuse, over-eating, under-exercising and to their shrink's chairs. At the battlefront, their colleagues call them "wimps and losers". Women have traditionally been the ones to stagger to psychologists first. But now my shrink tells me that more stressed-out men are seeking help, too. The problems are so intense that even we males have to admit something's wrong.

"We've seen them all," says my shrink. "They're so tired. They are better off going home and sleeping for an hour."

Where is everyone running to? Well, we know lemmings drive themselves off land and into water. I think cash-strapped corporate rats are trying to escape their monthly mortgage payments. Whatever the case may be, it should be no surprise that corporate misfits like me, end up becoming entrepreneurs. And hopefully, not transform into the big turkeys we once worked for. Amen.

# If You Work For A Turkey (2)
(or why I became an entrepreneur)
*By Babe Rat* ™

"You've got to train your boss," some weasel at work told me once. You can, he claimed, insult your boss in a hundred ways and still be his best friend.

Fine for him. His boss had a sense of humor. Mine was the original macho male who still thought he was God's gift to the planet, if not females.

Forget talent, hard work and lucky breaks. How you get along with your boss can make or break your career. Will your boss talk you up for raises, groom you for promotion – or is your success a threat to him or her? In the latter scenario, you might as well just get out, to another company or at least another department.

Your spouse, lover or family sees less of you than your boss. He can be a pit bull terrier, Saint Bernard or poodle. And what chance do you have to size him up in advance before you take the job? A 20-minute interview during which you're trying hard to sell yourself? First impressions are usually bunk.

One former colleague confided to me in the ladies room. "My boss is such a turkey," she said. "But if I get another job, I'll probably get stuck with an even bigger turkey." She re-applied her lipstick and concluded: "I might as well stay here."

I didn't have the same choice. My boss made the decision for me and I got what we in the pits learned to call the bronze or loony handshake. My weasel friend on the other hand, just went higher – because he had a good, kidding around relationship with his boss. He managed his boss; my boss managed me.

"There's some truth to managing your boss," says some fat cat working for a local management consulting company .

The trouble between bosses and subordinates are due to expectations from both parties: "The perfect boss is supposed to represent the best in the group – in every way."

The most perplexing problem bosses have is that they don't know why employees are so cold towards them. "When bosses attempt to break down this barrier by being friendly, some employees perceive this as an unwarranted intrusion."

It is sometimes easier for the employee to confront the boss (not mine). Employees seem to have more right to disagree and negotiate with their boss these days. But don't push your luck.

Bosses are supposed to be open and communicative. At the same time, employees expect them to keep their distance. But not so much that the boss is withdrawn and reclusive.

The most common complaint experts hear is that the boss is not listening to them: "When employees are patronized, they feel stupid."

Most employees are vitally interested in improving their relationship with their boss. And reducing their stress loads. Who's more likely to change — the boss or the employee?

The onus is on the employee. "When employees don't get along with their boss, they first do nothing and try to put up with him." Then they commiserate with their peers.

"What they need to do is examine their attitudes and values. Then change the ones that are causing the problem. Or try different strategies, aiming to communicate to the boss in a way he can understand."

Is that clear enough? Your boss won't change. You will. Change now or whine forever. Or start your own company and lure away his best customers. The turkey deserves it.

*(As for Babe Rat's corporate career, her outbursts in the boardroom eventually led to an involuntary job termination..)*

**The Old Boys' Club**

**The Old Girls' Club**

A good day in the life of Joe Rat, as corporate rat.

Now that his bosses were stuffed, Joe Rat often wondered what they would be like when they're roasted.

**Employees with Attitude**

**Babe Rat gets passed up for a promotion and tees off at work.**

13

**Why did Celine Le Friesen** [TM]**, former senior partner of Holstein & Holstein bare all for alien artist, Vince Van Kook (black velvet nude specialist)?**
**"The system milked me too long," says Ms. Le Friesen.**

**Joe Rat's exit interview at XYZ Corp.**

# From Employee to Entrepreneur

**Getting support from the family is important when becoming an entrepreneur. Any extra cash helps, too.**

Insomnia is known to run rampant amongst entrepreneurs. For Joe, counting sheep did nothing for his dreams. He's switched to counting money.

**A banker's worst nightmare**

**A good day at the bank for Joe Rat -
Lending rates plummet to zero!**

**Sharkie's Super Submarine Shop -**
**"Yeah, I wonder what kind of skeletons he keeps in his closet?"**

**There's no business like the manure business.**

**The trouble with being your own boss**

"Are you too tongue-tied to suck up to somebody?"

Then try Joe Rat's *tongue twisters*, edible aerobic suckers designed to relax weary tongue muscles. They come in 10-, 15- and 20-minute workouts in breathalyzing flavors, such as, minty mint, crazy bananas and chocoholic's chocolate.

.Joe's wife Babe launches *Rat Poison*, a deadly femme fatale perfume sought out by stressed-out female executives looking at clawing their way up the corporate ladder.

By day, Rose Lard teaches managers the fine art of boardroom quilting. By night, she works on a sleazy novel, *Life Would Be Better as a Bimbo.*

**Joe Rat goes to Hogtown to raise venture capital.**

**What do politicians do when they become entrepreneurs?**
**"They raise leeches."**

# In Business

**Entrepreneurs with Attitude**

**The hare makes a few bucks on the side.**

**Prince Charming's escort service -
where dreams *do happen*.**

Public lavatories get privatized.

**Crazy Chuck's Chili Bar -
cheap food and free gas**

**An alien adventure -
cow puts foot in mouth.**

Do cow patties fly?  Of course, they do.
Joe Rat's alien partner introduces a
biodegradable Frisbee to his home planet.

**Another case solved by the "CIA" -
Cow Intelligence Agency.**

39

**Pete's Perogy Palace -
Joe's brother opens a fast food kiosk.**

**The Joys of Consulting I**

**The Joys of Consulting II**

**The Joys of Consulting III**

**Entrepreneurs Anonymous**

**Bats from Hell courier service
- a real fly-by-night operation**

The phone snatchers are back!

Martian phone company enters North American market, luring prospective customers with free pizza. But are Martian pizzas for real? Can they deliver within 30 minutes or less?

47

**Garfunky's Hats takes off, as horny animals value their most prized body parts.**

**Green consciousness becomes part of every business.**

**Black and white fashion wear for young urban sheep appeals to the herd.**

Bovinism hit the sheep pretty hard. For once, the pigs followed.
It was great for the sheep's self-esteem and Bo's business.

**Hogtown's *Pigwet's* (that's Pig Latin for Wet Pig) hogwash scheme is no bull. Time-stricken urban hogs just don't have time to wash behind their ears.**

52

**Babe Rat opens up her own hardware store,
gender specific and politically incorrect,
for women without partners, sports widows, etc.**

An encounter at Babe's Hardware with super male model Two-Time Cody, a tall dark handsome dude. But rats, he's married to some young sweet thing.

*Mechano-Man* - designed for women by real men. For a household robot that does real work, try *Suzie Homemaker*, on back order by about six months.

# And they lived happily ever after.

**A miracle for Joe Rat -**
**Better than seven dwarfs are bored vacationing non-unionized elves from the North Pole. They agree to help Joe out from January to July.**

For clued-in readers, why no rats in this book have smaller ears or any tails.

**At a time of heightened animal dating rights, co-worker is stunned by politically incorrect comment.**

**Some things are just beyond a parent's control.**

**Sly Fly ™ gets burned by his agents dropping dead like flies on him.**

**Sly Fly hires first lady private investigator.**

63

Sly Fly's first lady private investigator busts **Buzz** and **Sting** on her first assignment. The rest is history. Sly Fly now only hires females and painted his office mauve and pink.

***Sweet Sox***, **soft enough for a woman, but designed for men by a real manly rat named Joe.**

Rose Lard finds a non-aerobic way to lose weight.

After 30 days, frozen leeches are pulled from grocery stores. Lucky for Rose Lard, who found that thawed out leeches could be re-frozen. One box was all she needed to reach her desired weight.

Rex's button gets fellow puny entrepreneurs whining.

To relieve the monotony of routine lipo-suction, Dr. Jekill goes *incognito* and becomes Dr. Hide on Tuesdays and Thursdays to perform facelifts.

Joe Rat pursues cousin Dr. Jekill/Dr. Hide for venture capital.

**A rich relative is a likely venture capitalist. The possibility this possibility this person may be a little crazy, may actually help.**

**Aaron, Sue and Sam (ASS) open their aromatherapy division with *Farmer's Perfume*.**

The competition takes another look.

**Word's out that *Farmer's Perfume* is a hit amongst female young urban sheep.**

To order: surf the Web to Joe Rat's home page. Key in body specifications and credit card number.

**Such is life in the oil patch at *Fossil Rock Bistro*.**

It's funny how the scum come crawling out of the woodwork when they smell money.

# Entrepreneurs - The Next Generation

**Beyond Reason** - marketing to Generation Z, today's purveyors of edible nerds, dweebs, gobstoppers and green snot.

When the son of an entrepreneur grows up.

**Ratilla** ™, **the 8 year-old daughter of Joe and Babe launches a weekend business. She quits after neighbor's hungry she-dog devours one of Ratilla's clients - a soft cuddly koala bear.**

**Joe Rat's Family - 20 years later -
Nepotism - what else is new?**

**Boy meets girl**

WELL, I'M GOING TO BE A LAWYER.
GOOD. THEN YOU CAN BE A GARBAGE WOMAN BY DAY. AT NIGHT, YOU CAN BE A LAWYER.
THAT'S NOT A REAL JOB BEING A GARBAGE MAN.
OKAY. I'LL RENT MYSELF A GARBAGE TRUCK AND A GARBAGE MAN.
BUT YOU STILL WON'T MAKE ANY MONEY.
THAT'S OKAY. AT NIGHT, I'LL BE A TAXI DRIVER.
COME ON. WHO CAN AFFORD CABS?
YOUR CLIENTS, OF COURSE.
Nattalia ©

**Life after death for the entrepreneur**

# Epilogue

In the end, Joe Rat is still the quiet little rat that he's always been.  In fact, he's even quieter because his pockets aren't filled with loose change that he used to borrow from B.Rat's piggy bank.

Of all the products, Joe Rat Inc. has made over the years, his aerobic suckers were his number one seller.  Customers had such an appetite for the original four-inch sucker that after the first year of sales, Joe released the eight-inch fat-free super aerobic sucker – at ten sucks per section, one is guaranteed to burn off 200 calories during one workout!

Joe's Surfwear was an instant hit amongst the web cruisers and cyberpunks.  There was no problem in selling *Sweet Sox* either, of which sales reached record highs last year.  Joe's latest clothing venture was developed by Albert in research.  Made from special high-tech materials, a peanut-sized pellet is zapped in the micro-wave to pop up into one pair of wrinkle-free disposable undershorts.  Yes, Joe is a rat of his word when he told countless males they would be rid of ironing (and washing) their undershorts forever!

Two-Time Cody [TM] who was a big attraction at Babe's Hardware quit to market his own home improvement video.  Some buyers were disappointed as Two-Time Cody is no longer the hunk he once was.  (He should be working out, not drinking cool ones.)

Babe just opened her 120th hardware store on Phobos, (the moon on Mars).  Her number one customer is Gina at Pizzabell (a former domestic engineer who is convinced she can put artificial intelligence into *Mechano-Man*).

Sales of Babe's *Rat Poison* have grown steadily and undergone several formula changes, including one that's unleaded.  Not to be confused with the target market for *Farmer's Perfume*, *Rat Poison* targets the executive elite.  Even though, entrepreneurship has taken off after years of downsizing, right-sizing and re-structuring, large multi-nationals have not died off entirely and neither have the turkeys that manage them.

Meanwhile, Joe's former employer, XYZ Corp. under a hostile takeover by ABC (alias All Better Company) Inc., bit the dust.  The turkeys he worked for, and who started up a New Age quilting bar, are now running a franchise of quilting shops for men only.

Rose Lard who started out in entrepreneurship as a management consultant, now lives in Los Angeles. Her romance novel, *Life Would Be Better as a Bimbo* has recently been made into a movie and translated into 20 languages. Ms. Lard's love life has also blossomed, even though she has refused to yield to lipo-suction or anything vain like that. Believe it or not, she ends up re-marrying Garfunky the Goat. As the horny animal population has been aging, Garfunky's hat business has also been thriving. His two-headed hats remain in popular demand.

Fido, the Rat family's dog, made numerous attempts in setting up his public lavatory service. He was forced into early retirement. Municipal officials shut him down for not procuring a city license.

B.Rat ™ makes big money. At 12 years, B.Rat started Pumpkin Computers. His lovable plush drool-proof machine-washable computers for infants, came in shapes of pumpkins, bats and witches. A year later, B.Rat expanded his operations into *Cool Computers*, a new line of computers that makes a fashion statement for teenagers. B.Rat's pocket-sized *Cool Computers* came in neon colours with built-in CD drives and screens for computer games. By 15 years, B.Rat made his first million dollars and began paying his parents room and board.

Horsing Around Co. lost its manure business to ASS Manure and negotiated a merger. There was a lot of hoopla as to what the new company could be called, like ASS Horsing Around or vice versa. It was settled to just call their merger A & H Manure Co. They recently underwent a plant expansion for *Farmer's Perfume* and quite frankly, those studs are now really working like horses.

Poliwog ™ shut down Prince Charming's escort service in cowtown to set up an oil company in Irian Jaya. He didn't find oil, but he found a lot of gold.

Fritz and Felix. Those two taxation consultants just had it up to their yin yang with regulations from the national capital city and called it quits. They now teach aquacize classes at Feline Fitness Centers, and are doing very well.

As for the fate of Crazy Chuck's Chili, Skip Boa, Bats from Hell courier service, Pigwet's Hogwashes, Runtel, Pizzabell, etc. – that would be another story altogether. Thanks for taking the time to enjoy this book. Joe Rat and his friends wish you all success in whatever venture you undertake. It could very well be ... another miracle!

Joe, I always thought you were an entrepreneur.
No, I was a corporate rat until I saw the light. After 21 years downtown, it was kind of a miracle!
Nattalia

# Miracles for The Entrepreneur
## Written & Illustrated By Nattalia Lea

*Cartoons for the overworked and underpaid. Book for giving at the office (whether you're the boss or employee), to friends, for birthdays, graduation, Christmas, or special occasions. Ex-corporate rat starts up some bizarre but profitable businesses. Come visit Joe Rat's world where pigs turn to lipo-suction for dieting, politicians become leech farmers, aliens drink purple milk and a couple of horses get taken over by a trio of asses!*

**To order, please use this coupon:**
*Check off number of books. Add on shipping and handling charges.*

Name: _____
Address: _____       E-mail: _____
City: _____       Prov./State _____ Postal Code _____
Tel: _____       Fax: _____

**Canadian customers:**
___ *Miracles for the Entrepreneur*        $14.00 + $.98 (G.S.T.) = $14.98 each
   **Shipping and Handling Charges:**     $2.99 first book, $1.99 extra copies

**International customers:**
___ *Miracles for the Entrepreneur*        U.S. $10.95
   **S & H to the United States:**        U.S. $2.50 1st book, U.S. $2.00 extra copies
   **Other countries:**                   U.S. $4.50 1st book, U.S. $3.50 extra copies

Send cheque or money order (no cash or CODs) payable to *Platypus Publishers* to: Platypus Publishers, 2323E 3rd Ave. N.W., Calgary, AB. T2N 0K9 Canada (Include shipping and handling with orders. Allow up to 6 weeks for delivery. **Thank you**.)